Listen

by
Ute Carson

YELLOW ARROW
PUBLISHING
Baltimore, Maryland, USA

Listen
Copyright © 2021 by Yellow Arrow Publishing
All rights reserved.

Library of Congress Control Number: 2021946574
ISBN (paperback): 978-1-7350230-7-6

Cover & interior art by Alexa Laharty (Instagram @alexaelisabeth).
Interior design by Yellow Arrow Publishing.
For more information, see yellowarrowpublishing.com.

Contents

Acknowledgments	1
Waiting for . . .	7
Then and Now	9
The House of Childhood	11
Center of the World	13
Flames Rising	15
Little Things	17
Hub of a Wheel	19
Ageless	21
A Snapshot in Time	23
Breaking Away	25
Crying is a Gift	27
Presence	29
Surrender	31
The Quotidian	33
Relic	35
The Past Lives On . . .	37
Cradling the Heart	39
Regret is Only for the Living	41

Relinquishment	43
Stars in the Night	45
Not Night Yet	47
Old Lovers	49
Living on Borrowed Time	53
Closing the Circle	55
Secret Anniversaries	57
Sacred Ground	59
Bleeding Trees	61
Death is Not One But Many	63
She Still Lives Here	65
Seasons of the Body	67
Echoes	69
The New Normal	71
Risks Around Each Corner	73
Unsung Heroes	75
Friendship	77
Small Pleasures	79
Two Love Stories	81
Magical Greenery	83

Ode to Water	85
The Wall, Monument to Disenchantment	87
Self and Others	89
Sleeping with a Cat	91
Wonder	93
Talking and Listening	95
About the Author	97

Acknowledgments

"Cradling the Heart"
Green Silk Journal, Fall 2018

"The Quotidian" and "Regret is Only for the Living"
The Pangolin Review, November 2018

"Ageless"
Scarlet Leaf Review, No. 3, 2019

"Relinquishment"
first appeared Thehealingpoems.com, February 2019
republished *Universal Oneness,* Author Press (India), Summer 2019

"Friendship"
Green Silk Journal, Spring 2019

"The New Normal"
Dime Show Review, Spring 2019

"Waiting for . . ."
Wordsmith HQ (United Kingdom), Spring 2019

"Breaking Away," "Crying is a Gift," and "Ode to Water"
Poethead, Word Press, April 2019

"Old Lovers"
Levitate (Chicago), April 2019

"Unsung Heroes"
Foliate Oak Literary Magazine, May 2019

"The Wall, Monument to Disenchantment"
published as "Over the Green Divide"
Indolent Books, May 2019

"Echoes," "Living on Borrowed Time," and "The Past Lives On . . ."
New Reader Magazine NRM, Issue 6, Summer 2019

"Little Things," "Relic," and "Stars in the Night,"
Literary Yard, June 2019

"Wonder"
Down in the Dirt, online June 2019, print March 2020

"The House of Childhood"
Plainsong, Hastings College Press, July 2019

"Sleeping with a Cat,"
Mustlovecats, July 2019

"Hub of a Wheel"
34thParallel Magazine, Issue 70, November 2019

"Not Night Yet"
Poetry Pacific, November 2019

"Then and Now"
The Fox Poetry Box, December 2019/January 2020
reprinted as runner-up in the TCK 2021 Poetry Award

"Talking and Listening"
Green Silk Journal, Spring 2020

"Secret Anniversaries"
Indolent Books, March 2020

"Death is Not One But Many" and "Magical Greenery"
New Reader Magazine NRM, Issue10, Summer 2020

"Risks Around Each Corner"
Yellow Arrow Journal (Re)Formation, Vol. 5, No. 3, Fall 2020

"She Still Lives Here"
Quail Bell Magazine, January 2021

"Flames Rising"
The Fox Poetry Box, February 2021

"Seasons of the Body"
Muddy River Poetry Review, Issue 24, April 2021

"Self and Others"
Expanded Field Journal, Summer 2021

"Center of the World," "Sacred Ground," and "Bleeding Trees"
The Flapper Press, August 2021

LISTEN

Waiting for . . .

Godot who never comes.

Or does he?
While we wait
with Vladimir and Estragon

a migrant girl picked up
at the border prays for protection
and is raped by her captor.

A young man fleeing violence
falters in the desert and
founders while he waits for help.

A Yemeni mother pleads for bread
for her starving child
who perishes while she waits.

Not all can be saved.

But as long as there are Good Samaritans
willing to comfort or rescue or feed,
waiting will not be in vain.

Then and Now

When I was young, fog enshrouded me.
I forged my own footprints
but paid little heed to their traces.
Now in old age,
as a bright sun pierces the fog,
I wish that years back
my vision had been clearer.
What can I do now?
If I was judgmental,
I now see life's complexities.
If I took love for granted,
I now love with wonder.
If I consoled sparingly,
I will now help shoulder sorrows.
If I was self-absorbed,
I will now attend to the lives of others.
I cannot spool time backward
but I can spin my intentions forward.

The House of Childhood

We return to the place
where we first heard voices,
smelled the air and tasted nourishment,
where hands caressed or frightened us,
where comfort was our cocoon
or neglect made us shiver.
The tears of harm are cold,
the tears of joy warm as a lagoon.
We carry the house of childhood within us,
and spying through its translucent walls,
we keep life at a distance or embrace it.

Center of the World

Cloaked in a happy childhood
the child is the center of its universe.
Parents, siblings, grandparents move around its orbit,
adding security, color and play,
and letting the child dream of
being a fireman, Batman,
riding a white steed
or donning red traveling slippers.
In adulthood the white horse
becomes a common sedan,
the red shoes sensible brown footwear,
and the dreams remain a childhood treasure
that has long been tossed
into the well of possibilities.
But at any time the treasure can be retrieved
by diving deep into the past.

Flames Rising

The fire is roaring, how did it start?
A layer of wood chips, rolled up papers, twigs and sticks,
then a match and the pile ignites.
Bluish tongues lick the wood
until a hypnotic flame,
symbol of transformation,
glimmers as it rises.

We all have been warmed by a fire we did not build.

Parents set a fire
that sends out sparks to dispel darkness,
and lights the way for the young into the world.
Parents tend the hearth,
manning the bellows when embers cool.
Children, thus warmed, will start fires of their own
and carry on the tradition so that flames can rise again!

Little Things

Memory sifts our experience in unpredictable ways.
Big events may get stuck in the mesh
while small happenings slip through.
In the spring of 1945 I was four and a half,
helping my mother earn extra food rations
by picking potato bugs
off of fresh green leaves in a farmer's field.
Because I was quick with my hands, my jar began to fill
with the yellow and black striped beetles.

My mother, picking just ahead of me, suddenly collapsed.
I rushed to her side, knelt and stroked her sweaty brow.
My grandmother, working an adjacent row,
was beside us in an instant.
After my mother was whisked away for an emergency appendectomy,
Grandmother took me home and stayed with me.

I clutched my catch tightly so as not to spill the little things
that were crawling halfway up the inside of the jar.
I dumped the tiny creatures onto the kitchen table
and tried to count them
but they quickly scattered, so I put them back.
I felt my cheeks flush with joy.
I had not lost a single one!

Hub of a Wheel

A secure childhood builds trust.
A child learns to love by being loved.
Nurture reflects and molds nature.
Seeds germinate in dark reaches of the soil
and burrow up to the light.
Greening tendrils need protection and care.
Grandparents can have a part in this venture.
They can relieve busy parents,
cradle babies, sing lullabies, tell stories,
and lend a finger to steady attempts at first steps.
Grandparents are allowed to indulge the young.
Shared laughter is unencumbered by everyday concerns.
Sunlight strokes the little shoots
and when stalks grow as tall as a horse's head,
grandparents' hearts brim over with joy.
With time's passing grandparents wither
and learn the lesson of letting go.
They may not witness the full flowering or
participate in the harvest of their offspring.
But they will know the satisfaction
of having been, for awhile, a hub
in the wheel of life.

Ageless

When I was little,
I didn't know that my grandmother was old,
that her white hair had once been raven black,
her face wrinkle free,
and that her voluptuous figure had lured
many a man from his righteous path.

Snuggled against her body, I was warmed.
Encircled by her arms, I felt protected,
her kiss wiped away every hurt.
And when she leaned over me at bedtime
her sweetness smelled like vapors of incense.
Above all, she taught me about love
with words married to her sense of what lasts.

A Snapshot in Time

When we look at an old person, what do we see?
A queen with gout,
a demented grandfather dropping his spoon,
a faded drunken beauty staggering off the stage.
We are blinded by the present.
How difficult it is to picture our parents as young lovers,
or the bearded homeless man as a smooth skinned baby.
It takes a leap of imagination
to peer through the fog of time
and see each stage in life
linked from first to last.

Breaking Away

Years ago at bedtime,
my grandson's chubby arms
squeezed my neck like a boa.
Now that he is growing up
my arms encircle him.
He squirms at my affection
and wiggles free from my embrace.
Then as his long legs stride out,
he glances back,
tossing me a smile.

Crying is a Gift

I dislike sentimentality
and have always thought
that tears should be shed sparingly
until one day our eight-year-old grandson complained,
"I don't like my friends to laugh when I cry.
How can I be happy again if I don't cry?"
Tears are our release
from joy and sorrow,
and like a stream
they gurgle over small stones
or gush over ravines,
all ending in the universal maelstrom
of lament and comfort.

Presence

You could barely reach my little finger
as you toddled at my side,
clutching my hand as we crossed the street.
Years later I pressed all my good wishes
into our firm handshake
as you strode out into the world.
Today I see you in my mind's eye.
I pull you back when
you walk through a sinister forest,
and urge you forward along a sunlit path.
Though I hover nearby I allow you privacy,
and don't disturb your dreams.
But along every byway, illuminated or dark,
I am present, invisible but real.

Surrender

I fret about my loved ones.
"Does it help?" a friend asks,
which misses the point.
My worries are uninvited guests,
but like any guests
they cannot simply be ignored.
Worrying is as involuntary
as the nightmares
that crowd my sleep.
I fight bravely against them
but in the end
I have to reconcile myself
to being tossed about
in tempests of unpredictability.

The Quotidian

The roulette of fate does not let you choose
the circumstances of your birth,
nor are the traits embedded in your character
of your own making.
But you can decide when and where
to step off the carousel of life
and take the wonder in.
I alight at the quotidian stops,
not the everyday places
but there where I glimpse an ordinary stone
glowing in the moon's watchful beams.
And then I get back on.

Relic

My grandmother's couch is stuffed with horsehair.
The fabric is faded and threadbare.
The old cushions have been covered
with fresh material on occasion.
Grandmother used to read her Bible
leaning into the upholstery.
Later on, my mother's knitting needles
clicked against the wooden armrests.
Still later, children and grandchildren
slurped from their milk bottles
well beyond babyhood and
bounced to the squeaking of rusted springs.
The experiences of loved ones
are traceable in the seams.
The couch bears the contours of past and present.
More than a cherished piece of furniture
it is a treasured keepsake of a family's life
woven through with nostalgia
for vanished people and times.

The Past Lives On . . .

Our grandson bursts into tears
as we dismantle our 18th century armoire
to pass along to the next generation.
"Its spot in your living room will be empty," he laments.
To comfort him we draw his attention
to the story the old piece tells.
"It has survived many generations," we begin,
and show him how it is held together
with wooden pegs and iron hinges.
He marvels at the carvings on the doors.
We look for the craftsman's initials chiseled into the facade
and run our hands over the ornamentation on its lacquered sides.

Many years ago, the armoire decorated a parlor
in the baroque castle "Bielwiese" in Silesia.
Until the onset of World War II,
generation upon generation was photographed in front of it.
After the war, a farsighted relative rescued it, loaded it
onto a cart, and hauled it to western Germany
from where it later left by ship for America.
It has belonged to us for nearly three decades.
Now it will find a home with one of our daughters.
The youngest generation will assemble
in front of it to be photographed.
History is embodied in such artifacts
and holds a place in the family of things.

Cradling the Heart

Chocolate hearts,
cutout paper hearts,
hearts of gold,
all symbols of the one heart,
sweet, malleable, and strong,
pulsing through a life's years.
But beware!
Unless you take tender care of it,
it will wither and die.

Regret is Only for the Living

Watching an artisan at work on a glass etching,
I suddenly remember my mother
teaching our children how to ornament glass bowls
with flowers and animal designs.
I never thanked her for her efforts,
and the children took her patient instructions for granted.
How pleased she would be, these years later,
to see me admiring the intricate configurations on the bowls.
Alas, the gratitude is mine alone.
Regret is only for the living.

Relinquishment

When years ago my mother-in-law
bemoaned the fact that
to stay steady on her feet
she had to exchange
her stylish heels for flats,
I shrugged off her complaint
as a small concession to growing older.

Now that it's my turn
to scale down to comfortable shoes,
I realize that parting with my heels
is more than a minor inconvenience
and may be a kind of dress rehearsal,
preparing me for my final leave-taking
which I will undertake unadorned.

Stars in the Night

I remember many delights.
Riding my mare bareback across a meadow,
my naked toes brushing the tips of dew-moist grass.
Waking up in my lover's arms,
feeling my heart race.
Cradling our baby,
my breath caressing its fox red down.
All these precious moments glimmer
in a starless night.

Not Night Yet

It is evening, the night still at bay,
enough time to stroll with a loved one
through a colorful garden
as leaves begin to fall
or pluck an apple or two
from an overripe orchard.
Before sunrays fade to darkness
a few daylight hours remain
to recall stories about a life
shared, complex and rich.

Old Lovers

They are folded together like a blanket,
desire strong as ever
though the flesh is weak.
They sink into each other's warmth,
savoring the tenderness welling up
from a life well lived together.

Living on Borrowed Time

When you are old
you live on borrowed time
as the sand in the hourglass trickles through.
Now is the time to reclaim experiences
you pawned in the past.
Give memories new life
by sowing the seeds of your stories
in the fertile green minds of the young.

Closing the Circle

What drew us when we first met
across ocean, class, and culture?
His adventurous spirit?
My desire to move out and away?
What I know
is that my heart made up its mind
the moment he stood at my door,
in that old beige raincoat, drenched.

Over the years,
we stumbled across rough terrain,
and sailed on smooth waters,
with hands intertwined
or fingertips barely touching.
The center held.
Now, cradling this dear man in my arms,
I feel nothing but gratitude.

Secret Anniversaries

There is something different in every aching heart:
Awareness of death
as when a butterfly landed in the palm of my hand,
wings heavy, baked by heat, flailing.
Awareness of failure
as when, betting all my money on that spotted horse,
my fortune seeped through my fingers like sand.
Awareness of loss
as when I stormed into the night fog
after a blustery quarrel with my partner,
her words icy darts; "I don't love you anymore."

There is something different in every jubilant heart:
Dawning of love
as when through flickering candlelight
sparks ignite in recognition, and we are on fire.
Dawning of beauty
as when breast milk sweet as honey
becomes an amber river
that nourishes new life.
Dawning of freedom
as when there is no longer the need
to place feelings under a bell jar
but to let them shine.

When the last anniversary dawns on the horizon
I hope to celebrate with few regrets but
much gratitude for a wondrous ride!

Sacred Ground

I kneel and place an ear on the mossy carpet
covering my mother's grave.
Closing my eyes against distractions,
I hear the earth whispering.
Out of the deep darkness
my mother's life comes back to me.
As the noonday warmth reddens my cheek
I rise and memories of her bloom in profusion.
I honor my mother by brushing
leaves of grass and tears from my face.

Bleeding Trees

The wind of mortality
sweeps through the woods,
stripping away leaves
and downing limbs.
Sap turns to bleeding tears.

Visible still on a trunk,
the outline of a heart
carved long ago.
Now time spreads a veil
across this emblem of long-lived love.

Death is Not One But Many

None of our animals die afraid.
A vet comes to the house
where our old cat gets her sleeping potion
while curled up on my lap.
Our ancient mare sinks to her knees
between brushstrokes while munching carrots.
But what of the dog hit on a busy road
with no one there to end its misery?
And on the human spectrum, who does not envy
the composure of a Dietrich Bonhoeffer,
walking unshackled to the gallows,
face tilted toward the heavens?
And yet, what about the little girl in the desert,
crouching at her mother's side begging, "Mama wake up!"
when a sip or two of water might have saved her?
Or captives, hands bound and heads pushed to the ground,
pleading in vain for mercy from vengeful swords?
The German poet Rilke wished for every person
a death of their own following a life well lived.
Death as surcease, accidental death, death as fruition,
needless death, malevolent death.
Death is not one but many.

She Still Lives Here

My wife and I occupied this house for 55 years.
My parents restored it following the Great Depression.
We have shared the cooking, the cleaning,
kept the yard trimmed and the roses flourishing.
When the sun streams through our tall bay windows
the laughter of children and grandchildren
cascades along its golden beams.
When the rain pelts the shingles on the roof
or a storm rattles the wooden shutters,
we remember huddling together during hard times.
Although the old house is showing pockmarks and wrinkles,
echoes from our lives reverberate from cellar to chimney top.
When my wife died six months ago
lucrative offers from realtors rolled in.
But I can't leave. She still lives here,
along with all those who came before us.

Seasons of the Body

Youth is spring,
blossoms, smoothness, idealized perfection.
Old age is winter,
frost, concealment, farewells.
Only summer and fall build bridges,
ripeness and golden harvest time
gliding toward wilting and letting go.
Through different lenses we may see
the lustrous skin of youth as cold as marble
while wrinkles of age show warmth and wisdom.
Young eyes may shine bright and proud,
but lack insight.
Muscular legs can run fast,
but be unable to slow down and meditate.
Dark locks of hair entangle in an embrace,
while silky gray strands are caressed by the wind.
The firm body finds admirers,
but tenderness hovers over frailty.
The young heart beats with optimism,
but may neglect to open its chambers to listen.
If we accept our bodies, ourselves across time,
we find beauty in every season.

Echoes

We live in each other like Russian dolls;
only our contours and edges are soft.
The shells in between are translucent
and memories resound through the spaces around.
My lover's footsteps reverberate from his bed to mine,
and I feel the temperature of our embrace.
Saliva pools in my mouth from his succulent kisses.
I smell my mother's straw blond hair
and the mossy sour breath of my babies.
My grandmother's fingers tenderly comb my locks
and my father walks toward me erect and whole,
unmarred by wounds of war.
Life stories are recorded in the crevices of my brain
and emotions bounce back from hollows in my body.
I am filled with the echoes of my loved ones.

The New Normal

If we are fortunate enough to survive
all matter of bodily insults
and land relatively unscarred in old age,
we may believe that we can live like that until we die.
Then life teaches us otherwise.
When my young grandson challenged me to a footrace,
I didn't hesitate,
despite the seven-decade difference in our ages.
(Had I not been a sprinter in my youth?
The dash from starting blocks was imprinted in my mind.)
I bolted confidently forward, only to fall flat.
My body could no longer oblige.
Other infirmities have become constant companions.
My doctor tells me that this is the new normal.

Risks Around Each Corner

"Nothing can be taken for granted when you're 80.
There is risk wherever you turn."
My doctor's warning echoes as I leave the clinic.
Even well-oiled hinges are beginning to creak,
my heart is skipping a beat,
and my feet burn at night.
Getting through an ordinary day saps my energy.
I am drained after even a leisurely walk.
But should I stop dancing because I fear a fall?
Should I leave off lovemaking
lest pleasure stop my heart?
No longer climb a little higher
because I'm short of breath?
Now in old age I pay for excesses of joy
with mounting aches and pain.
But rekindling the thrill of cherished skills
still seems worth it, all in all.
By staying connected through breath and touch
we delay the long sleep that awaits us all.
I have resolved to take risks
while I'm still able to savor life's sweet nectars.

Unsung Heroes

In our house we know where the sofa is,
and the television and the comfortable chair.
We're familiar with the color of our walls.
Our inner furnishings, though, are hidden from view.
Our organs make themselves known only when distressed.
They break their silence when the liver swells,
intestines cramp, or kidneys fail.
Leaders among them, heart and lungs,
hold honored positions.
They are the Givers of Life.
And the nervous system gets credit
for its tireless communicating.
It's the army of foot soldiers—
pancreas, spleen—diligent companions
who keep us functioning unawares,
performing their tasks like clockwork.
They are seldom bathed in the warmth of appreciation.

Friendship

Come with me to a Texas meadow in the spring
and take in the sight of
yellow Agarita, white/green Milkweed, purple Asta.
Rest your eyes on the gorgeous Bluebonnets
with leaves the shape of thimbles
and the creamy orange Indian Paintbrush,
honoring Spanish botanists.
Shall we call the myriads of beautiful flowers our friends?
Some we gaze at from a distance,
some we pluck and press in a book,
some we bind into a bouquet,
from others we collect the seeds.
Their colors bewitch us,
their fragrance pleases our noses,
but only one flower is picked
and gathered to the heart.

Small Pleasures

For Christmas I got a big shiny red apple,
a box of marzipan, and a bag of roasted nuts.
We were poor back then but we gathered
in the cozy holy atmosphere by the fireplace
where my grandmother told stories
and my dad sang carols in his mellow baritone.
Though I envied my friend Max his new bicycle,
his potbellied stove stood cold
while his parents quarreled on Christmas Eve.

Later in life, I dreamed that my books
would appear on bestseller lists
and reach a wide audience.
Instead, little magazines picked up my stories,
and readers of my poems were few in number.
Still, when I received a personal word of appreciation
or a favorable review, I found my path,
though not paved with gold,
strewn with flower petals.

Two Love Stories

We hear of two folktales.
One tells the story of a little mermaid,
the other of two childhood friends, Gerda and Kai,
separated by an evil Snow Queen
who deadens Kai's heart with an ice splinter.
The mermaid and Gerda are on a journey in pursuit of their loves.
They bring gifts, determination, and devotion to their quest.
The mermaid is fated to a life of longing and sacrifices,
her love forever unrequited.
Gerda experiences the transformative power of love.
Neither woman is preoccupied with herself
and neither shun the arduous journey and its trials.
When the mermaid finds her beloved, he does not recognize her.
Gerda enters the kingdom of the Snow Queen
and melts the ice in Kai's heart with a tear.
Both heroines retain the purity of their souls.
The foamy swells of the sea hide the mermaid's bleeding heart.
She links arms with her sisters as her prince sails out of sight.
Gerda takes Kai back with her to warmer climes,
her devoted friend at her side once more.
Two love stories, both universal,
one uplifting, the other tragic.

Magical Greenery

My unruly ivy, left unpruned,
snakes over the walls of my house.
A snail inches along a tendril,
and red-breasted robins dart in and out
of the deepening, widening foliage
that shimmers in shades of aquamarine.
Touched by the sun,
raindrops cold and clear slither from leaf to leaf.
Night robs the thicket of its colors
and silences the bees.
But when light and warmth return with the dawn,
butterflies flutter about.
Nature thrives in abundance.
Onlookers wandering by may wonder
who lives here, hidden away
under this mantle of magical greenery.

Ode to Water

I am a nymph,
I inhabit the rivers, lakes, and streams,
sing to brooks, the ocean,
and dance to life therein.
I rise as a mermaid,
an aquatic creature,
drown fires,
quell the thirst of the earth,
mix with the air.
The moon is my lover,
together we balance
the rhythm of the tides.

The Wall, Monument to Disenchantment

A man stands, arms tightly clenched across his chest,
and the child retreats.
The man opens his arms wide like wings,
and the child jumps into his embrace.
A woman shears the hedge between backyards
as a neighbor ambles up on the other side.
Their words pass easefully over the green divide.
When a boy throws a rock hard against a wall,
it boomerangs back and hits him.
When he skips a flat stone across a shallow creek,
droplets lightly sprinkle the water's surface.
A girl from here meets a boy from there
on a bridge spanning a great river.
They talk and laugh and touch,
surprised at how much they have in common
and enchanted by their differences.

Self and Others

How do we venture into the lives of others
and still remain true to ourselves?
We demarcate relationships
between teachers and students while learning,
between counselors and clients while conversing,
between doctors and patients while healing.
We build barriers, high and solid,
wire fences between properties,
erect No Trespassing signs for emphasis.
But we also plant hedges
for words to travel across, even handshakes.
I prefer flexible boundaries.
My favorites are the ones made of rope
that I can climb over or crawl under.
When I get snagged by a thorn or a twig
I retreat and regroup.
We all have sensibilities
knitted together by nerve tangles.
There are narrow openings in the knotted web
where messages can slip through.
It takes persistence to burrow through the mesh
and reach a waiting heart.

Sleeping with a Cat

I tried to teach Bazaar, our big orange tabby,
to snuggle at my back or lie on my feet,
but he chose my hair as his favorite resting place.
Nose buried in my sparse locks, he purrs
as his soft paws massage the soft strands.
On cold nights he warms me
and on hot summer evenings I swelter under his weight.
Come morning, Bazaar is my alarm clock.
He stretches his supple limbs, nudging my forehead with his.
I do my exercises in bed as he looks on,
tail curled around his hindquarters,
head erect, ears perked.
He waits until I turn off the house alarm,
then dashes out into the still dark dawn.
From our bedroom window he leaps to the fencetop
and sets off on his morning rounds in the neighborhood.
As the coffee machine percolates
we hear him scrambling up the cat ladder
my husband built on the other side of the steep fence.
Now comes breakfast which he relishes at leisure.
Then, depending on the weather, he ambles onto our porch,
eyeing flocks of birds landing on out-of-reach feeders
and hisses at the clicking taunts of squirrels.
Occasionally a lizard or a fledgling becomes his prey,
but at day's end his nightly routine begins again
as he curls up in the nest on top of my head.

Wonder

Christmas 1944, our last festivity on native soil.
Refugees are streaming westward.
Two months later we will be among the fleeing.
Russian troops have set fire to villages nearby.
The bridge over the river below our castle is destroyed.

But our devoted forester lumbers in from the dense forest,
as he always does at this time of year,
his shoulders sagging under a blue spruce
which he places in the parlor.
My mother and grandmother decorate the evergreen.
I am four-and-a-half.

On Christmas Eve, the large French doors swing open
and I am spellbound by the sight
of a tree with candles ablaze.
"Did the angels bring us all this light?" I whisper.

Now, years later, the childhood magic settles
like stardust on my aging eyelids
and I dream of that Christmas Eve
when wonder was my reality.

Talking and Listening

An old man prattles on
about driving across country in a Model T Ford
in his twenties.
He tells about traversing the parched desert
and being robbed at gunpoint at a gas station in Nevada.
A therapist listens to a recovering addict
and nods approvingly at his progress,
then lends a sympathetic ear to a battered woman.
Talking is about self, listening about others.
The talker is a storyteller,
the listener an interpreter.
Like inhaling and exhaling,
we need both.
By exchanging stories,
we can reach understanding.

Ute Carson, a German-born writer from youth and an MA graduate in comparative literature from the University of Rochester, published her first prose piece in 1977. *Colt Tailing*, a 2004 novel, was a finalist for the Peter Taylor Book Award. Ute's story "The Fall" won Outrider Press' Grand Prize and appeared in its short story and poetry anthology, *A Walk through My Garden*, in 2007. Her second novel *In Transit* was published in 2008. Her poems have appeared in numerous journals and magazines in the U.S. and abroad. Ute's poetry was televised on the Spoken Word Showcase 2009–2011, Channel Austin. A poetry collection *Just a Few Feathers* was published in 2011. The poem "A Tangled Nest of Moments" placed second in the Eleventh International Poetry Competition 2012. Her chapbook, *Folding Washing*, was published in 2013 and her collection of poems, *My Gift to Life*, was nominated for the 2015 Pushcart Prize. *Save the Last Kiss*, a novella, was published in 2016. Her poetry collection, *Reflections*, came out in 2018. She received the Ovidiu-Bektore Literary Award 2018 from the Anticus Multicultural Association in Constanta, Romania. In 2018, she was nominated a second time for the Pushcart Prize by the PlainView Press. *Gypsy Spirit* was published in 2020 as was her essay, "Even A Gloved Touch."

Ute resides in Austin, Texas with her husband. They have three daughters, six grandchildren, a horse, and a clowder of cats. Connect with her at utecarson.com.

Thank you for supporting independent publishing.

Yellow Arrow Publishing is a nonprofit supporting writers that identify as women. Visit YellowArrowPublishing.com for information on our publications, workshops, and writing opportunities.

www.ingramcontent.com/pod-product-compliance
Lightning Source LLC
Chambersburg PA
CBHW020543080526
44583CB00013B/963